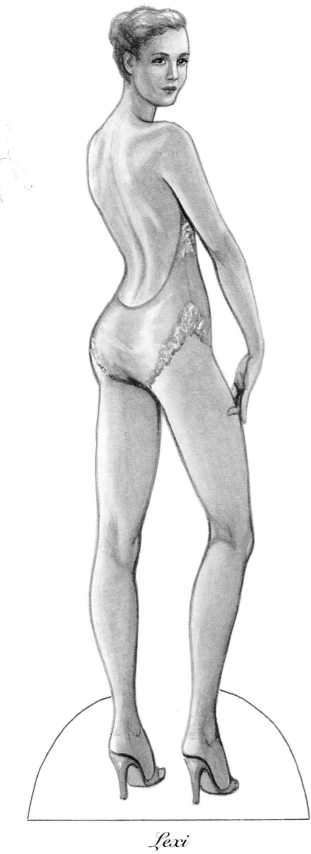

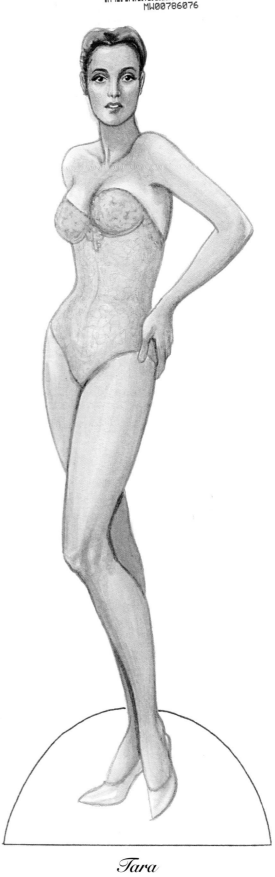

Lexi

Tara

PLATE 1

Glue ends of strip to
back of shoulders,
leaving center free. Slip
costume over doll.

Glue to back of
hairstyle and slip
over doll's head

T

Glue ends of strip
to back of skirt,
leaving center
free. Slip costume
over doll.

Do not cut out
spaces between
arms and body.

T

T

Sixteenth Century Iron Corset

Versace Evening Gown

PLATE 2

Glue ends of strip to back of skirt, leaving center free. Slip costume over doll.

T

T

T

T

ca. 1660s "Bodie" Stays

Versace Dress

PLATE 3

Glue ends of
strip to back of skirt,
leaving center free.
Slip costume
over doll.

Glue triangle
to back of
hairstyle and
slip over doll's
head

Do not cut out
space between
arm and body.

Glue to back of
hairstyle and slip
over doll's head

T

T

Eighteenth Century Stays and Panniers

Vivienne Westwood Dress

PLATE 4

Do not cut out space between arm and body.

Early 1880s Corset and Underwear

Christian Lacroix Evening Gown (front view)

PLATE 5

Do not cut out space between arm and body.

L

Glue to back of hairstyle and slip over doll's head

Glue ends of strip to back of skirt, leaving center free. Slip costume over doll.

L

L

1880s Victorian Ball Gown

Christian Lacroix Evening Gown
(back view)

PLATE 6

Do not cut out space between arm and body.

Glue to back of hairstyle and slip over doll's head.

T

Glue ends of strip to back of shoulders, leaving center free. Slip costume over doll.

Glue ends of strip to back of shoulders, leaving center free. Slip costume over doll.

1890s Underwear and
Sleeve Crinolines

A Maya Hansen Design

PLATE 7

Do not cut out
spaces between
arms and body.

Early 1900s Corset

Corset Dress

PLATE 8

Glue ends of strip to back of waist, leaving center free. Slip costume over doll.

Glue to back of hairstyle and slip over doll's head.

Glue ends of strip to back of knees, leaving center free. Slip costume over doll.

Do not cut out space between arms and body.

T

T

T

1920s Front-lace Corset Girdle

An Oscar de la Renta Design

PLATE 9

Do not cut out spaces between arms and body.

Glue to back of hat/hairstyle and slip over doll's head.

T

T

T

1940s "Waspie" Waist Cincher

A Christian Dior Design

PLATE 10

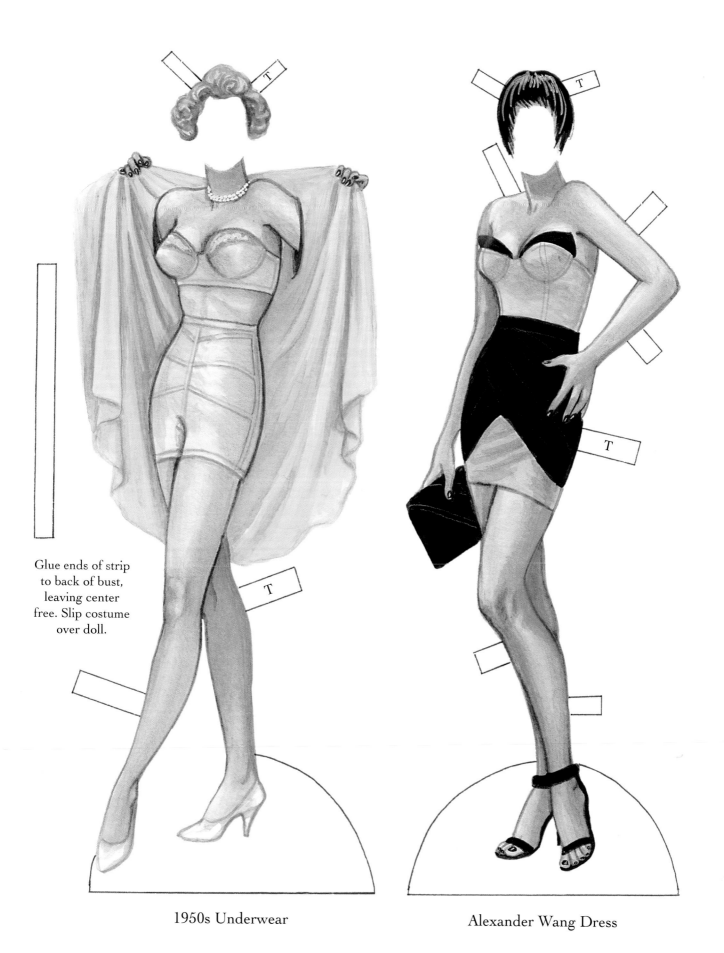

Glue ends of strip to back of bust, leaving center free. Slip costume over doll.

1950s Underwear

Alexander Wang Dress

PLATE 11

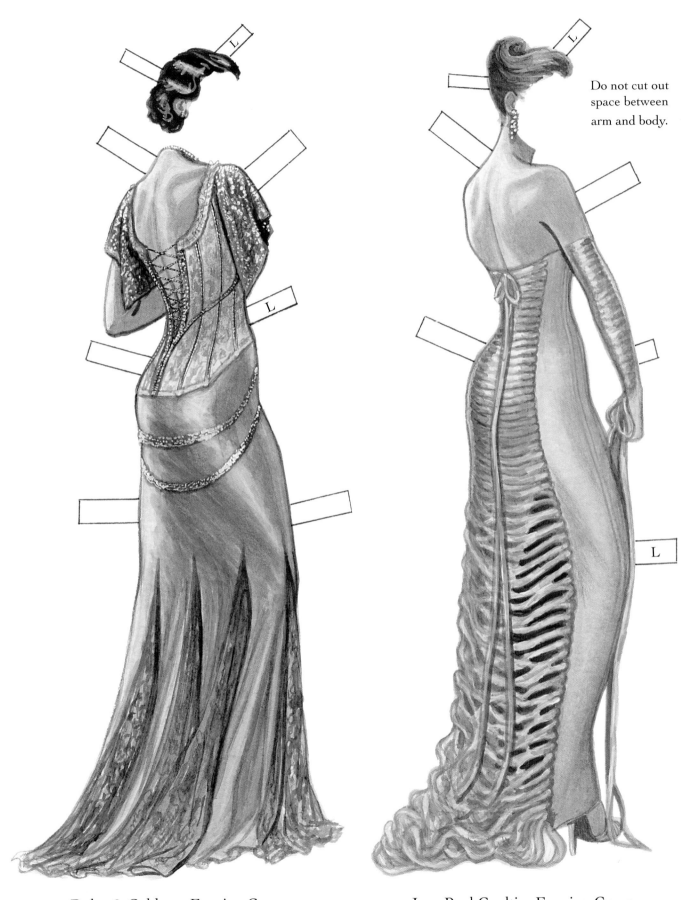

L

Do not cut out
space between
arm and body.

L

Dolce & Gabbana Evening Gown

Jean Paul Gaultier Evening Gown

PLATE 12

Do not cut out
space between
arm and body.

Glue ends of strip to back
of skirt, leaving center free.
Slip costume over doll.

T

T

Justin Alexander Wedding Gown

PLATE 13

Glue to back of
hairstyle and slip
over doll's head.

Glue to back of hat and
slip over doll's head.

Glue to back of hairstyle
and slip over doll's head.

Dolce & Gabbana
Dress

Lady Morgana Dress

Thierry Mugler Jacket

PLATE 14

Glue triangle to back of hat and slip over doll's head.

M

M

Michael
Corset for Men

Dandy of the 1830s

PLATE 15

PLATE 16

Modern Dandies